Slack Land

Slack Land

Poems by

Kris Spencer

© 2025 Kris Spencer. All rights reserved.
This material may not be reproduced in any form, published,
reprinted, recorded, performed, broadcast,
rewritten or redistributed without
the explicit permission of Kris Spencer.
All such actions are strictly prohibited by law.

Cover design by Shay Culligan
Cover image by Julie Spencer
Author photo by Mat Smith

ISBN: 978-1-63980-804-5

Kelsay Books
502 South 1040 East, A-119
American Fork, Utah 84003
Kelsaybooks.com

for Brian Patten and Ted Kooser

Acknowledgments

Some of the poems in *Slack Land* were previously printed in the following journals:

Amsterdam Quarterly: Port de la Chapelle
Bombay Literary Magazine: "Slack Land," "Haunted by Cats," "The Chances of Margot"
Drawn to the Light Press: "Yearning Sonnet", "Home as a Series of Opening Lines for an Unfinished Sonnet About Time," "Truth Sonnet"
Every Storm Is a Message (novel): "A Father Tells His Daughter a Tale of the Sea to Help Mend Her Broken Heart," "A Young Mother Tells a Story to Her Daughter Who Cannot Sleep for the Sound of the Waves on the Beach"
Full House Literary: "A Line on a Walk"
Halfway Down the Stairs: "Holes"
Hyacinth Review: "Bound"
Mediterranean Poetry: "Is That So Bad?"
Reverie: "Home as a Series of Opening Lines"
Ropes Literary Journal: "Fisherman's Bar"
The Marrow Poetry: "Written for a Grasshopper"

Contents

Preface

Part 1: In a Landscape

Slack Land	19
Little Metal Ball	21
I Feel Something Is About to Happen	22
Yearning Sonnet	23
Grass Whistle	24
Fox Hour	26
Dune Slack. Scarp Slope.	27

Part 2: Everything Is Luminous

Heaven's Gate	31
Holes	32
Bound	33
Vacation	35
My Daughter Wakes Up	37
A Different Blessing for My Son	38
Animal Sounds	39
We See Colours	41
Fool's Sonnet	42
A Fool's Reply	43
A Father Tells His Daughter a Tale of the Sea to Help Mend Her Broken Heart	44
Home as a Series of Opening Lines for an Unfinished Sonnet About Time	47
Scars	48
Lost Guitar	49
Leaves	50

Part 3: A Pot of Brushes

Splitting Ions   53
Notes in Preparation for an Ink Drawing of
    Flying Ants Before a Storm   55
Stopping   57
A Blue Ship with a Red Sail   58
Truth Sonnet   60

Part 4: Delicate Circles

Written for a Grasshopper   63
When the Last Leaf Falls   65
The Chances of Margot   66
Arabesque   67
Waiting for a Wealthy Friend Who Doesn't Show   69
For the Night   70
no lines   71
Is That So Bad?   72
Duck's Eye   73
Porte de la Chapelle   74
White Cat   75

Part 5: Bone Trilogy

Line on a Walk   79
Vertebrae   81
Counting My Bones   83

Part 6: All the Possibilities of Water

She Misses Her Husband   87
Waiting, Uncertain About the Future   88

Mermaid	89
Fisherman's Bar	90
Morning in the Backyard as the Sun Rises	91
A Shelf Is an Open Line	93
A Hand Is a Hollow Bowl	94
On the Downs	95
After a Storm, Fishermen Go Back to Sea	96
Out with Her Husband at Dusk	97

Part 7: Love That Passes By

Change of Season	101
On the Beach	102
The Season Changes	103
Who Has No Land Has No Sea	104
Late Spring. New Town	106
Sputter	107
A Young Mother Tells a Story to Her Daughter Who Cannot Sleep for the Sound of the Waves on the Beach	108

Preface

When I pick up a poetry collection, I usually let the book fall open and start reading from the middle. I suspect the poetry gods are used to it by now. Still, I thought it might help to share that this collection has a gentle narrative arc. The poems aren't dependent on one another—you can start anywhere, and no harm done—but if you do choose to read from cover to cover, here's a rough guide to how the story unfolds.

Part One is about youth—a boy growing up. In *Part Two*, he reaches adulthood, finds love, and starts a family. *Part Three* follows him as both a father and an artist. *Part Four* focuses on his children as they begin to see the world with adult eyes of their own. *Part Five* turns inward—a kind of reverie on the body, and how a visual artist connects anatomy with consciousness. *Part Six* follows a more distinct storyline: a daughter returns to the family home on the coast and falls in love with a fisherman. In *Part Seven*, she has lost him. Moving on, she takes their daughter with her to a new town.

I wrote these poems after finishing the first draft of my debut novel, *Every Storm is a Message*. There are connections—shared words, shared stories. In terms of some of the themes of painting and life on the coast—while I've never been a fine artist or illustrator, my dad was one of the best. I watched him work as much as he'd let me. In the same way, I can't sit on a fishing boat without turning a little green, but my wife's family has made their living from the sea for generations. I've spent many summers in Normandy, trying to understand how salt spray, fish scales, and trawlers shape families and communities—these things certainly fixed something special in my wife.

I know my kids as well as any father does, which is to say, with the same feeling as a cowboy hanging onto the mane of a rodeo horse. They have sand and pearl in them, that's for sure.

Part 1:
In a Landscape

Slack Land

Walking through the bracken,
down to the river, I tell my children,
it was dead back then—proud
to have lived the cobbles
that were once furred and slick.
The dead water came from
the mill. The smell was like
wet paper and drains. Now
there are ribbons of weed
in the current, caught with minnows
and frogspawn. Green holds
in the air around us, and the smell
of soil. I tear up turf from the slope—
a blanket of sods we once laid
over green branches
to make dens.

This was how we played
in the Slack Land. I see
how my son's eyes are bright
to be where I once was. I am good
at walking on this old ground.
I don't slip on the rumps of waxy
forest grass. I pick a long bullrush
and split it, show my daughter the stem
filled with white sponge. The path
to the weir is blocked now.
The boy died. He was in my year.
The water is a spell—
it draws you down. Falling

onto the wet stone, his broken
body carried off to the still pools
under the bridge. The same year,
a girl I kissed at a party caught
a cramp and drowned in the cold water
of the quarry lake on the hottest
day of summer.

Coming back to this place
to see how I am still
snagged in its thorns
and wire. Moving through
the ivy, we find an old works
at the break of the slope with mossy
stones around a tunnel entrance
that makes a cave. We don't get too close.
It'll be haunted, I say. Out of time,
it has become like an amphitheater.
My daughter pirouettes and bows,
happy that all the ghosts are mine.

Little Metal Ball

my grandpa gave me
a ball bearing

I held it in my fist
all summer

running through
the fields

it left a smell of blood
on my palm

the holding
dulled the metal

perfectly heavy
I depended on its

round weight
like a planet

I would have given it
to Eleanor Bell

when she kissed me
but I lost it

playing silly devils
by the river

I Feel Something Is About to Happen

Measles, mid-August

The warm rain has passed across the town
washing away the dust and clutter of

late summer. Sunlight comes sharp through
the curtains. Outside, my friends are playing

banshees, running wild with the dogs. The sky
is a bowl. Looking out, there is a girl

in a white dress sitting on the swing.
She is wearing her mum's sunglasses, they

keep slipping down her nose. Jumping off, she
runs to catch up with the rest of them. In

the evening, outside seems full of meaning.
I watch the girl hold her sister as the

air begins to chill. She has plaited black
hair and she drapes it over her sister's

shoulder. I think how it would feel to have
that braid on me under a different sky.

Yearning Sonnet

How in the songs it is always hid deep
inside, but I wore mine on the surface,
like acne. I thought, *this will end soon*: how
different I will be after. I fell in
nettles, all stung up, the warm hives buzzing
like reckless kisses—the body electric
humming in the wires. How the birds were mute
then. The older girls would grab at me, and
take kisses because I was fair game.
I waited, rubbed up. It only takes a
little time to be loved. I learned my body—
no wounds that needed healing could be seen.
I would walk shirtless in the sun and step
lightly, heart holding what my hands could not.

Grass Whistle

it is just a
thin
shiny thing
slick as
metal

I taste it
as it catches in
my mouth
and sticks
there

you know
I need
a little
sharpness
sometimes

to cut
a fingertip
on a
blade of
green

and pull
it tight
between
thumb and
thumb

making
a grass
whistle
that sounds
out loud

Fox Hour

There were monsters—
shadow monsters in the blue-glass day.
Where did the noise come from?

Heartbeats, shallow breaths—steps
on gravel. When the light changed
from over the bridge

you leaned in and missed my lips,
banging my cheek.
It didn't hurt

or leave a mark.
You sang to me, then.
How heavy did the night come down,

dull as old tin.
What showed? A few toes
of late summer hanging

over, the grass moving
with a sound like water.
The finger shapes in the dark,

and how it went for me—
your red hair,
soft as fox tail.

Dune Slack. Scarp Slope.

Even this far into November there are bumblebees shaking the heather. He opens the wine. It tastes of green apples. They can hear the waves but cannot see the water from this low spot surrounded by the crests of dunes. Behind them is all the jumble of the scrub: the blackberries are finished, and the gorse is weathered to dull grey, but the sedge and bell heather are still in flower. The wind is up in the marram grass. It is warm now, lying against the slope of the dune. They have the best of the weak sun. She reaches out and places a hand under his jacket so that she can feel his shoulder through his shirt. He rolls on to one elbow so he can look into her eyes. Her face has flushed a little from the wine. She can see a light pulse in his neck. With his fingertips he traces the contours of her face, and she turns her head towards him so their lips touch.

The light dims as she walks home. She takes the path past the dark church through the graveyard, climbing the steep slope of the chalk escarpment. There is no clear way, and the stiff grass and thistles of the clumped ground are slick so that she sometimes reaches out for a handhold on a low hazel branch or hummock of dogstail. Reaching the boundary of the farm, she wriggles under the barbed wire fence and walks on past the dark barn with the timothy grass growing up. Between the wavering edge of day and dusk, the valley is a blue gulf. Colours deepen. Small flies bite as the daylight goes down. Stars fasten up above the pale glow of the farm, rounding the night beyond the boundary fences and the dark trees. Everything looks mute. The falling night takes the colour from the world so that skin is same as water, same as sky.

Part 2:
Everything Is Luminous

Heaven's Gate

You could look into my heart—
a car park, flower meadow,
the cliff-top path
white with broken chalk and flints.

You saw this before?
—No, it was something else.

Heaven stays quiet
when we have no shoes,
when we can't find the door.
The gods prefer their boats
moored in perfumed harbors.

With you, I've grown rich—
picking berries in the dunes,
juice staining our fingers.
Sometimes there is lark-song,
down from the sky, and the hiss
of waves on the beach.
The world is half land, half sea—
sand rattles, grass sings,
insects whirr like machines.

I know this feeling—
always with me,
always different—
like a lark rising
from the weedy stubble,
or eating raspberries
ripened by the sun.

Holes

I am thinking of planting a tree
now the soil is warm.
March is when
the spade
does not ring or jar
against flint and frost
but goes in soft
through the earth—
like a sigh.

You tell me:
don't make holes
that cut roots
and move things
laid down before
—let the ground be.

So, we leave the ferns
under the maple,
the faded sunflowers against
the bright wall we built.
Soft earth has its own way
of holding.

We walk old paths,
feel the pull of seasons
as the ground hums
beneath the mulch.

This tree
will keep our time
in its rings.

Bound

Books press. You've reminded me of
that moment when, as a reader, I decide
to go on. When I know the words will

take me somewhere. Like they were ladders
up against a wall. Black ink on white paper.
Zipper teeth meshing the soft fabric of time

occupied. I will go on with you. I will
open my dusty life and be the fine dust
swerving in a sunbeam.

Books span. You've reminded me of
that moment, when, as a writer I decide
to continue. All the similes. The empty

paper, receptive as an unmade bed. The first
mark creating disorder, as if a child had
stamped their foot on the surface of an icy

puddle or dropped a pebble into an ant's nest.
Words that are bridges over rivers, the gum
between our fingers. I will stick with you.

Books bind. You have reminded me of that
moment when the light is going as the sun
falls, and everything is suddenly luminous.

And the world is new, again, even as night
comes. How moths replace wasps, and birds
gather. Where words press. How we need

to move for them to touch us. To let them
settle, not grab or trap them in a net. I will
watch you fly and hear your words.

Vacation

We don't need to stay in one place.
Or celebrate by singing or reciting
a poem. Framed: our son crouching under an oak,
our daughter in a slow waltz with me—

years of toys hanging on the door. When I
saw the cat, I asked why its white fur had
dark patches. You said, *it crawls under cars
and sleeps on the stove top.* That was then.

At the station, our children watch. There is
a tall man, his girlfriend on tiptoes
for a kiss. An elderly lady says to her young
companion: *Is this a greeting, or our last goodbye?*

The man's fingers rest on the girl's bare
arm, hers are pressing into his cheek.
There's a boy, with his handsome mother,
counting all the men with brown shoes.

The teller is matching receipts against her takings
for the day, she catches the eye of the man
selling papers. The kingfisher colours flashing
off his kiosk: cyan, orange and white.

Like a film, our son says, as he slides
shut the carriage door checking with us
it's OK. He strokes the yellow veneer and reaches
up to touch the rope netting of the luggage rack.

They both draw together, sharing the wooden
crayons: canal swing bridges, the fat
shoulders of the hills. We eat strawberries, fresh
from the punnet and watch the landscape change.

My Daughter Wakes Up

She reaches out her arms and legs—
so she can be a star,
the points of a compass.

There is the cool rub
of the cotton sheets
against her skin.

The weight of the quilt,
the feathers inside crackling,
as she kicks it off.

She feels all the sand and salt
of her night, her dreams hanging
like pollen in the air.

A Different Blessing for My Son

Here, you make marks on white paper keeping
the colored pencils neat in a plastic tub.
Your lines are like lightning strikes. Hunched at the

thin desk in the front room, you are taller
now than the rose bush I planted when you
were born. I hold your hand and it is thick

and broad. You are already an artist. You don't smile
but you are happy with your picture. When you
draw, I see my father. Back in his small flat,

with his wooden board on his knee as an
easel, criss-crossed with score marks from his
Stanley Knife. Hunched over, nodding his head to

an old song on the radio: *Love, oh love,*
oh careless love. He told me: *You can draw a bit,*
but you'll never make an artist. That was his blessing.

Animal Sounds

Our daughter jumps
from the fourth step
of the stairs,
just to be caught.
Sitting in the crook
of my arm
I feel her breath on my ear.

    In the hour before dawn
    two foxes are rooting on the street,
    bold in the dark. Their shrill barks,
    like babies crying. It wakes her.

Bringing her back
home, when she was
two days old—you said:
Don't worry

    She climbs up into our bed to tell us
    the story of her night. Suddenly
    wise. You ask her, *What good does it do*
    to be scared of foxes?

We are houses,
sometimes.

    Nose under tail, we share the pillows.
    I get up and open the velux. There is enough
    cold air pressing on my face for me to feel
    I am outside. I hear the low coo of the wood
    pigeons, *I DON'T want-to-go,* like my dad
    taught me.

There is a phrase of
my mum's that I thought
was lost.

> We stay awake. The sun up
> but not yet bright.

We sing to the breaking day.

We See Colours

Sweet silent thought
and summer's green.
Magpie in her tree.
A nest with five eggs.
Black tail flashes
green. Green leaves.
Eggs are blue-green.
Blue lobster turns red
in the pot. We crack
the claws. White meat
shines. On the table
in the green bowl
a green Comice pear
with a brown spot.
Look: it's like Eve's apple.
Lips and cheeks
come red as cherries—
from playing out
in the evening air. The bird
catches the violet light
of the sun's eye.
Everything we need
is here, sitting at
this brown table.

Fool's Sonnet

Considering things that grow up like plants.
How shallow trenches stretch out in war and
rage, turning flowers to frayed and tattered stumps.
We hide, ashamed to count all we lost and

broke—the last tree. We walk in bootless
grace as fools, regardless of what has been,
and what has gone. Fools and fools again to
be happy not to see the things that grow.

Why did you promise such a beautiful day
for me to leave the house without a coat?
There are no marigolds here, or tall sunflowers—
just a bare field and the damp of autumn.

How cruel to have held a precious thing and
break its stem like it were a cut flower.

A Fool's Reply

I didn't know the chill would come so fast.
The sun looked golden—how was I to know?
It never crossed my mind you'd trust my word,
and leave your coat behind to risk the cold.

We never mean to ruin what has grown,
thinking roots will hold, or that they can heal.
We cover things in dirt and call it care,
not seeing how the rot is setting in.

You speak of marigolds—I see them too,
but only for their shape, the color's gone.
I didn't mean to make you walk through thorns.
I thought the field was safe enough to cross.

You say I crushed the thing you tried to save.
But I just held it wrong. I didn't know.

A Father Tells His Daughter a Tale of the Sea to Help Mend Her Broken Heart

There was a young fisherman who fell in love with a girl, wild as the ocean. Every morning, as he sailed, he watched her gather seaweed from the beach. She would look out for him as he left, and wave. Each day they became closer. One evening, she was waiting for him on the quayside when he returned from the sea. They kissed without ever having spoken. It seemed that their happiness was set. As a token of her love the girl gave him the knife she carried at her waist. It was her most precious thing.

The next day he saw a seal lying on the rocks. Thinking of the dowry he would need to marry his love, he crept up on the seal, and unsheathing his love's sharp knife he plunged it deep into the beautiful animal. The poor seal cried out in rage and pain, and slipped into the waves taking the knife with it, down into the deep ocean.

The fisherman was angry. For the skin of the seal was beautifully marked, and shone like silver. It would have sold for a fortune, and given him the dowry he needed to marry his sweetheart. He was angrier, still, to have lost the knife which was his love's prize.

The next day he looked for the girl at the quayside but she was nowhere to be seen. He had wanted to tell her of the loss of the knife, and ask her forgiveness for his carelessness. As he searched in despair, a man approached him. Without any words the man placed a hooded cloak of sealskin on the fisherman's shoulders and with steely arms held him as he plunged off the quay into the waves.

They fell deeper and deeper. The fisherman feared he would drown but to his amazement he found he could breathe in the salty water. He could not break free. He was dragged far below the waves to a hidden cave. On entering he saw a hall full of beautiful creatures, half-seal and half-human in form. In the middle was his love, with a terrible gash in her side. Her eyes were closed and she was silver-pale. A cold dread came over him. He felt deep remorse for his cruel actions, even though they were made for love. He knew now that it was he who had so brutally injured her, and he feared that she would die from his hand.

The stranger who had kidnapped him from the quayside now held up the knife so that the blade shone, and passed it to him. He said, "Fisherman, I brought you here because you are the only person who can save your love, my sister. Only your hands can close the wound."

In this faerie place, the fisherman found the courage in his heart to step up to his dying love. Knowing nothing more than hope he gently pushed the wound closed with the knife that had dealt the mortal blow. To his great surprise, the wound healed over. His love opened her beautiful eyes and for a moment she returned to her human form and held him.

He was then taken up by the same steely arms and returned to the quayside. In the morning, nothing remained of his love but the knife she had given him. For once injured in this way, and saved by a human hand, no Selkie can return to the land. The knife, etched with love and pain, never left his side, and for his span of years he stayed alone among all the business of life—and he never harmed another seal lest he did violence to his lost love.

Home as a Series of Opening Lines for an Unfinished Sonnet About Time

I hold to the passing of time, with the
cat scratching at my pillow. A tired heart
is walking on the hill. I pass through the
persimmons and the ferns. Often, I have
gone this way before. A cold cry, from out
on the street. Waiting beside the window,
looking out. And the day is filled with sand
Home is the perfect day, with the wind in
the trees. Slow time brings a steady hand, and
the light in your eyes. The buildings are never
coming back, and the rest are falling in
the yard. I guess this is the passing time,
like an animal looking for a home
that hangs outside and won't be shooed away.

Scars

Hearts and anchors,
half-moons.
I have old scars,
faded now—
from barbed wire fences,
concrete edges,
missed throws
and broken branches.

Scars held like prayers
and promises.

How they change—
the marks we leave
and carry.

I tell my children:
things might fade,
but nothing
ever really disappears.

They know
my next scars
will be different.

Lost Guitar

rain comes down hard
filling the high gutters
spilling down

in the garden
with a clatter
on the cushions

that should have been
put away for winter
birds rattle in the eaves

ragged
feathers up
heads down in their necks

we look out
grey roofs
white birch shining

road running empty
light through the leaves
brings in green

making the loft
a forest
there is a time

in a storm
when the world throbs
like a bass line

Leaves

I use a wooden board to press leaves
into mounds. The piles look like giant tortoises
peering into the flowerbeds. Bunched seeds

hang from the branches of an old ash.
Some fall, like keys spinning over the wall.
A black collie runs and crouches behind

me, herding the loose leaves as I load
the wheelbarrow. I stop to look at my work,
one arm across the rake. The dog sits

and waits. You have put a plate of thick sandwiches
on the table. Your hair is brushed down. The light
comes warm through the window. You see a burr

on my sleeve. We don't talk about love anymore,
but it is around us. The dog barks at a pigeon,
pecking at the fallen apples, we call to him to hush.

Part 3:
A Pot of Brushes

Splitting Ions

Painting the curve
of the chalk hill as if it were
the rounded heft of a giant's
shoulder. The hatched blue
of the sky, the corduroy
strips of the fields; the sea,
powder-green—all lit with
the lustre of mussel shell.

I have a little Zinc White
mixed in my palette,
something of the blurred tones
of the horizon—where the ocean
meets the land. Like light split
through the lace of a bride's
veil, or the glow coming off
a clay pot on a warm day.

      ***

Waking in the night.
The wind is moving
in the old maple.
Behind the sound of
breaking waves, there is
singing in the air.

Looking out I see the fields
dancing with a blue light
coming down from the sky,
like a shower of cobwebs.
The sheep's ears are glowing
violet and the shed roof seems
rubbed with luminescence.

All over the bright fields,
there is the flicker and glow
of St Elmo's fire—like small
lightning, too fantastic
to paint. I watch for an hour
until it fades, leaving
the fields silver-grey
in the moonlight.

Notes in Preparation for an Ink Drawing of Flying Ants Before a Storm

Movement is the source of all change
  —Paul Klee, *Creative Confession*

    An artist returns home with pen and
      ink (the journey)
    Waiting there is a child with a bright
      smile (the light)
    There are flying ants in the air, they
      fall and lose their wings (flux)
    Later the warm air becomes heavy
      and there is a storm (energy released)
    In the field below, a view of a swollen
      stream (flow)
    Fish swim away in all directions (dots
      become lines)
    Before falling asleep the artist thinks back
      to the day and is glad (balance returns)

Empty paper waiting to be filled is receptive as a breakfast bowl.

    When making the first mark, consider ( ) all the
    choices ( ) and the chosen alternatives ( )
    and what it is safe to choose ( )

The first mark creates disorder, as if a child had stamped their foot on the surface of an icy puddle or dropped a pebble into an ant's nest.

The line rolls along the white paper like mercury.

What follows is a drive to return to
stillness and order.

When I open the door there are already ants in the air. They settle on the white flagstones, looking like Japanese calligraphy. My daughter comes to me and says, *Look, see how their wings come off when they land.* They are so sleepy and confused, it makes her giggle. She tells me: *They're looking for their queen.* Big raindrops come down. We see them on the path. Far apart at first, then they join up. We run inside, our clothes sticking to us, suddenly cold in the squall. When it stops we go out and the ants are gone, all washed away down the storm drain.

Stopping

I put my work away
in a narrow drawer,
waiting for the air
to be still.
In a moment,
the space becomes
round, and circles back,
like a cinematic loop.

Looking out towards
the brightest things
in the southern horizon,
I see Jupiter and Saturn
low in the sky.

There is not much to ask,
I am happy
to keep watching—
not asking
or thinking
how things
should be.

A Blue Ship with a Red Sail

In the harbour, a little girl is sitting next to an artist, to watch him work. He draws the outline of a seagull for her with just five strokes of his charcoal. He passes the sketchbook and a pencil to her. She draws a cat. It is good. The legs are four slender triangles and the tail curls up like smoke. He tears out the two drawings from his pad and gives them to the girl. She runs off, too shy to say thank you.

The artist meets his dealer in a pretty café. They sit outside at a wooden table. The dealer opens the book on the first page. She is careful not to bend or tear the paper, which is thick and creamy. The first drawing is of a tea-table standing in the corner of a garden with breakfast laid out. Behind the garden wall are fields and there is a copse in the background. There is some colour in the picture. Paint has been placed to show the baked brown of the cob loaves on the table and the blue rings on the milk-jug. On the next page there is a landscape. To sketch the scene, he seems to have pushed his gaze through a wire fence to show a path snaking up over the Downs. There is no paint in this picture but he has written, *pale as lard*, next to a part on the hill where the chalk is exposed.

A few times the dealer puts her hand gently on a page as the artist is about to turn it to indicate she has not finished looking. They do not speak. Everything looks fresh the way he has it. The composition of each picture is beautiful. He has drawn a bedroom as if he was standing on a chair in one corner. In a harbor scene there is a web of lines that become masts or rope-lines, nets, or the lines of the quayside runway.

Here he has written, *stiff like wire* and *up like bullrushes in a chalk stream*. In another, he has suggested a breezy upland by showing a spread of flowers in the foreground, their cups bent from a rush of wind.

The little girl comes back. She passes the artist a folded piece of paper. There is a round plaster on her finger. She stays to watch him as he opens her present. The girl has drawn a blue ship with a red sail. The artist smooths it out and places it in his portfolio. He looks at her to check this is what she wants. She climbs up on the spare chair. The dealer buys the girl an orange soda. She makes it last an hour. The little girl turns the pages and thinks of the colours she would add to the artist's pale drawings.

Truth Sonnet

I know a few things to be true. That in
time some things harden and some soften, like
food left out too long. And that we mostly
miss things on purpose: like an unopened
letter or a ringing phone lying ignored
in its cradle. Bees and flies come in through
the same open window—we kill one and
save the other. All God's creatures, after all.

I know my children's lives, and how my life
is now. I remember the triangles
of my childhood. Between is cracked and hard.
Maybe, as I lie dying it will warm
and soften. And the colours will be bright,
like the paint of my life was not yet dry.

Part 4:
Delicate Circles

Written for a Grasshopper

A thread of cloth hangs loose
from the stall's awning—
flies spin around it
in delicate circles.
There is a girl crouched
on the quayside,
looking at a grasshopper.
It hops six times—like flat stones
skipping on a pond,
or the way raindrops
make dust pop.
Across the harbor—two brothers
with a hosepipe are teasing gulls
feeding on fish-guts in the pallets.
The birds fret and flap,
but stay—they know water
too well to scare.
Crouched, the girl listens
as the grasshopper sings,
its green legs strumming the air.
The eldest boy is suddenly serious;
handing the hose to his brother,
he remembers the money
they were given
to buy two mackerel
for lunch.
They hear the grasshopper,
and smile over
to the girl who lives
on their street.

The grasshopper jumps away—
but it doesn't matter to the girl.
She hums a melody,
soft as wings—
half-laughing, half-hopeful—
hopping to land
in the quiet space
that the grasshopper has left.
The boys race
along the wharf, back
to their mother.
Their laughter fades,
until it is swallowed
by the space, and she is left
with the rattle and scrape
of the canvas stalls
as the wind comes up.
Standing against
the push of the breeze,
she feels the cold
through her dress:
summer is leaving now,
and so, the click and whirr
of insects in the grass
will stop. She wishes
the boys had stayed.

When the Last Leaf Falls

With her sister dying, she gathers
golden threads from her mother's
sewing basket. Each day, she walks
to the sycamore in the Square
and ties back the fallen leaves.
Her friends join in—
and then the whole town.
Autumn passes. The leaves turn gold
but stay until the warmth of spring
brings new buds.

Twenty years pass. Returning
from the city, she finds the tree taller—
its branches shading the top windows
of the Town Hall. Dulled and tarnished,
the threads still hang from the twigs.
Her sister's children dance in the Square.
Unseen, she watches their hands
reaching up
before she turns
and walks away.

The Chances of Margot

You might think that there is no need for chance
to begin things. That the steady turn of the
universe simply spins things out: one action

leading to the next. Like butterflies that
flicker and twist in the breeze. You might look in
a mirror, or rob a bank. You might wave

at somebody to have them wave back. Stretched
out in a wheat field with the light going, the ground
still warm. Where is the best place to smile? You

could fill your pockets with coins or pebbles
so that you rattle when you walk. The soft
rituals we use. The pad and the pencil. The

catastrophic molt of penguins. There is a siren,
out from the edge of the city: a fire engine
carrying chance, to someone else. You sit,

dropping matches in a cup. Legs crossed
in an old skirt, looking down the straight
street waiting for the next thing to happen.

Arabesque

Passed the grinders and pitchmen—
Dimitri, the anti-gravity man balances,
one-handed. His blocky muscles
bunched tight as fists, he slowly turns
his chest and lowers one leg
to stretch into an arabesque.
As he dismounts and bows, his eyes
are lowered to the crowd
as if in reverie.

The ringmaster calls:
The Flying Colombos and Maria.
Maria strides slowly to the centre
of the ring, pausing after each long step.
She loops a rope around her foot,
and with one arm outstretched
is hoisted up. She wears a weighted cape
with a blue star. Unclipped, it falls
in fast circles like an angel.

Behind a litter of pins, hooks,
chains and ropes, the other performers
are smoking under an awning.
They look older now.
Their leotards are patched and worn.
Dimitri is in the corner, powdering
his neck. He seems smaller. His gold
tooth glimmers weakly in the half-light.

Maria watches the ropes—
the wire-song of memory stretched tight.
She thinks, *I will open my arms and reach*.
She pulls a strap under her chin
and spins, head arched back, as she
is lowered back down to the ring
The damp sawdust is soft under her
kid-leather pumps. She is everywhere
in that moment as the spotlight fades.

Waiting for a Wealthy Friend
Who Doesn't Show

after Meng Haoran (689–740)

Dusty sunshine
   fades the day like old film
   with the blue bleached out.
There are crushed cans around the bin—
   scratched silver
   like lottery cards.
Exhaust fumes come up from the street,
   sour with ozone.
On the kerb, a smiling man
   sells hot dogs from his cart.
Last year, you said we would meet here.
   I have thought of the expensive things—
   the food, generous and heavy.
Now, the yellow taxis shuffle as the lights change.
   I sit with the tourists on the steps
   and watch the night come down.

For the Night

after Du Fu (712–780)

Empty streets. The cars are dead hulls, all grey.
Two white shops glow behind half-closed shutters.

Their light catches a spiderweb hung with pollen
and empty insect casings. Darkness and shadows,

what they hold—sometimes chance, sometimes chill.
Turning, turning, I am paper caught in an eddy.

Sky-held, rising and falling, I hold to the long watches
of the night before the dawn comes and stirs the cold air.

no lines

the frayed edges
of dusk catch
the hang-nail

of a broken day
as we watch
a satellite

shining
bright as a planet
the sky sinking

at the sea's edge
nothing is sharp
in the dark

are we moving
together
or falling apart

we hold to the
edgeless spaces
and turn away

Is That So Bad?

This is the place of giants
and dwarves; you might grow
or shrink here. There is the smell
of the sea and grilled meat.

Music floats like cigarette smoke.
The dunes are breaking, shifting
and falling; the sand won't hold without
the stiff grass. Wooden shack door—

I touch the handle. Waves blow in, oily
with lotion, and seem to catch fire in the sun.
People come here to wait. As if their
choice had meaning. Is that so bad?

If your slender frame is broken, why
not right here? What if a volcano comes
with ash? Would our powder mix and sink
down to make new rock on the ocean floor?

Was it water that came first or did
the carbon rise up like pollen? Three
flights up and bent like a supplicant
in prayer. Where is truth's bud buried?

Duck's Eye

*Inside, we're ageless. And when we talk to
ourselves, it's the same person we are
talking to, the same age, as when we were
small, and it's the body that's changing
around that ageless centre.*
—David Lynch, speaking to Mark Cousins

What energy do things have?
A room is empty
or people are dancing.
One is two,
the other is seven.
Electricity has a bigger number than water.
If there are too many paintings, or music,
that would be ten—
too much.
But if there was someone quiet,
just standing there, it could be OK.
It might be beautiful.
Low and high.
You can see how things are set,
like a duck's eye in its head.
Above the S-curve neck,
the body and bill—
as if the eye were a jewel.
To have sharp focus
for things in a life.
All you have done,
brought together—
like music.

Porte de la Chapelle

Inspired by the photographs of Myr Muratet

his dreams are boats
in this watched city
they put spikes in doorways
a concrete pyramid
   in a window well
the benches are round
he wonders why
they want to make
this place of dreams
   a sprung trap
he has never seen
the sea he wants to cross
he remembers goats
   perched in
   olive trees
   staring out
sleeping on cardboard
beneath the underpass
there is always
the movement of the trains
like waves crashing
everyone is covered here
his turquoise coat
and pink shawl
   tied in the Tuareg way
he has his father's face
   lined by years of searching
his mother's hope
   hidden in a scarf

White Cat

In a walled garden, under a round maple tree, sits a
white cat moving its tail in silent calligraphy.
   to see things and then move away

The stiff branches of the tree are green with moss. The
white cat walks away over white stones.
   to be sometimes scared of feeling

Can anyone go into the night like a cat and not be
haunted by all the phantoms of the day?
  to be caught by the fear of things going

Sleeping in hedges and walking the line of thin fences,
to find opportunities in the songs of foxes.
   to look beyond

And come back, narrow head nudging fingers
for food, fur up and wrinkled.
   to welcome another's love, again

What are the ghosts in a cat, and the twisted branches of
a tree, or the cry of a fox in the dark morning?
  finally, to be open to the world

Part 5:
Bone Trilogy

Line on a Walk

An active line on a walk, moving freely, without a goal.
A walk for a walk's sake.
—Paul Klee, "Initial Plan for a Section of the Theoretical Instruction at the German Bauhaus"

You might take a walk along a line, the line would always lead you somewhere. The line might be drawn on paper or on a road. It could be a smell, or a song in the air.

I.5

THREE CONJUGATIONS

active: *I sing* (the man is happy
and his mood is buoyant).

medial: *I hear the song* (the man's
heart falls to the axe-stroke of beauty).

passive: *The song is gone* (all is
quiet and the man loses his way and falls).

When the song is gone sometimes it leaves the echo of a simple rhythm. A repetition from left to right, or top to bottom. Like walking.

B   As we walk what is the relationship of muscle to bone?

One bends, the other stretches.

Bone matter is caught by tendons and ligaments and shifts as
 the tissue of muscle contracts.

> *A bone on its own does not move.*

II.22

The tightrope walker carries a pole.

When a body moves it is not free
it is caught.

> He calculates the gravity of
> the ends by becoming the scale.

Overloaded through the heavy dark.
He stumbles and makes
a correction.
His foot sticks, tied forever to the Earth.

Ligaments
stretch,
tendons tighten.

He falls.

Vertebrae

Along the lower way, gravitating towards the centre of the earth, lie the problems of static equilibrium that may be characterized by the words: 'To stand despite all possibility of falling'.
—Paul Klee, "Ways of Nature Study"

The rebel stands on
the flatbed of a Toyota
pickup and fires
a bullet into space
that spines up and
slows;
    it turns,
and falls back to earth
with an energy
that is harmless

The dull report of a gun is
small and hard as bone

a human body
half winged / half imprisoned
    by movement

the intricate mechanics
of structure
    so perfect

we might think we are
standing as God
The father of the bullet is the thought: *how*
              do I expand my reach?

The mother of the bullet is a movement: *I stretch
                         muscle tight from bone to bone*

the Rubik logic
of vertebrae
that click and crack
    infinite
with possibilities
and hold straight like
keystones that pivot
and do not topple
easily

          The refugees hear the machine-gun
          clatter of what might be bones
              falling
          and stand straight and
              still
          in the stiff spine of the checkpoint
            bones stay

Counting My Bones

Some bones can be felt: *sternum mandible pelvis patella*

The cage of ribs is sprung like the frame of
a bed or chair. Each bone is a question and
a prayer.

>My daughter draws around her hand
and traces where her bones belong.

>As a child I put on my father's jacket.
It hung loose on my small shoulders.
I knew his bones from my bones.

Bones get broken.   My nose was broken by
If your nose is hit hard   a boot, a head,
it will most likely   a wall. One way
break. It doesn't hurt   it went, then
so much. You feel   the other,
  confused. As if the   until it found
blow released   its fat middle. Like
       a fog.   a tree root.

I don't know how all my bones
are held. I know the exact position
of the bones that have been hurt.

Fashion models follow their pelvis—
everything else back-slanted.
The photographer tells them:
Stand like your body is broken.

When I was younger
I led with my right shoulder—
three bones: *scapula, clavicle, humerus.*

Now I try to stand straight
    with
    all
    my
    bones
    stacked
    like
    wooden
    blocks.

Part 6:
All the Possibilities of Water

She Misses Her Husband

She stretches out in the tub. The water
is milky with soap. She can make her body
disappear if she sinks down. Lifting an arm out
of the water, she is tanned, her muscles
are long from swimming. She presses
at the soft skin of the water, so different from
the surface of the sea. She has the stories
her father told her when his mood was good:
The sailor with ivory fingers who, believing
he had heard a mermaid, jumped beneath
the boat never to be seen again; the boy,
having befriended an octopus and growing
six more arms, took to living in the shallow
water beneath a pier and tying fisherman's
lines together—tugging at them so they'd pull
each other into the harbor when they thought
they had a fish. As she rises, her hips shift
the surface of the water. Some of it splashes
onto the tiled floor. She uses the pointed
end of a thick towel to wick up the spill
and pulls up the bath plug by its metal
chain. As the tub empties, the water leaves
a line of grit and sand, like the creeks
on the mudflats when the tide is out.
She thinks: *I am an empty boat,*
floating adrift.

Waiting, Uncertain About the Future

I sit on the hill's knuckle, as dawn
comes up. The farm below is hushed
like a sea cave—somewhere to be safe,
to listen and watch. In the light shade
of the green maple, I watch the sunlight
catch the feathery edges of leaves that
sparkle like light on the sea.

There is a crowd of starlings in the meadow,
holding still between the legs of the sheep. No bickering
over worms: just silence. They are waiting
—hiding. A falcon is hunting, wheeling in the sky.

Using the sun as a shield, it folds its wings and
drops—taking a juvenile by the wall. Settling in the maple,
it tears at the head—dropping the beak, that lies like a
yellow darning needle on the path I climbed.

The day feels pressed under a heavy thumb.
I hear the blood in my head as the sheep pull
at the grass. My thoughts drift out on the music
of things, to where the land meets the sea:
the crisping waves flare with red and yellow,
a mole-cricket sings in the grass.

My world hums with endings.
I wonder why happiness slips away
unnoticed, and how love
sometimes stays.

Mermaid

I lived in the heart of the sea—carried
like a gull, sometimes above the swell,
shifting then stilled; sometimes sinking
into waves, marking time on the flat shelf
of the shore caught with mud and shells.
The sea was my hair. As I swam,
I left circles in the sea's skin—
like the blue rings an otter makes
when it dives.

Here, the floorboards creak
beneath my feet as I dance
to the radio's throb—
Love, Oh Careless Love.
I know what it is
to leave the water and move free
but lose the music
of breaking waves.

Fisherman's Bar

In summer, you can tell if the fish are fresh on the ice of the stall if there are wasps drinking from the thin mucus of their eyes. Never whistle in the harbor, it will bring storms and worse than that. The wind comes in like a fist, like muscle. The waitress is tall and thin, with the teeth and skin of a recovering addict. They say most fisherman die at sea from urinating over the side, balanced on the gunnels at night, and losing balance. It is not so easy to climb back in a boat from the waves, even a little crabber. Not a nice way to die, scratching and kicking, getting cold and heavy with your trousers round your ankles as the water pulls you down. The seagulls fly down and peck at the fish guts in the pallets. When the tide is low, the sloping mudflats show on both sides of the harbor. You can see the buoys and their chains lying flat above the waterline. The boats look like cows lying down before the rain comes. There are gulls picking at the sand and mud. A speckled juvenile finds a thick bloodworm in the sea moss on the sea wall. It has hold of one end and shuffles its feet to stretch it thin before pulling it away from its anchor, and swallowing it whole. They serve the coffee hot and acid-sharp. I drink mine and try not to make a face: as if I were a tough fisherman.

Morning in the Backyard as the Sun Rises

I sing to myself
moving around the barn.
In my legs, the white cat
I found half-drowned
and starving by the bridge.

It growls at flies
that spin in the ragged shadows,
and chases the wasps and bees
in the meadow.

I tilt to the smooth moon
of my life. Things feel new
again. The resin-smell
of dust and shavings
from the sawed wood
we used to fix the paddock-gate.

Sitting on a tree trunk,
eating breakfast.
The cat jumps up
and nudges my arm.

I watch the mist move up
the valley sides, pushed
by the warming sun.

In the time it takes to drink
a glass of milk, still warm
from the cow, the mist thins
into wispy tails
which in a moment split
and melt to nothing.

A Shelf Is an Open Line

I collect things found in fields and along
the shore—for how they carry
what the world was. The flat shelf
of my windowsill is a clock of forgotten things.

Time is caught in shells and fossils—
old bones, branches
weathered blond by sea, metal bits
from worn-out machines. They stand in whorls,

piled like cairns, an open line
of chosen things. For how they feel in my hand
—smooth or ridged. I mix wood with metal, shell,
bone, a few weathered coins. Shaping space,

objects shift: some are covered, then return
—like a child finding a marble
half-buried in soil, still cold and round,
already fitting to the palm.

The shelf frames fragments—salt-streaked
coins, polished bone, driftwood,
fossils from deep earth and flat beach—
all salted and warmed by the same sea, the same sun.

A Hand Is a Hollow Bowl

My hand holds without keeping:
a bowl for fragments and found things,
placed and passed. It might scoop an ocean
or measure the sky's span.

I carry dirt and weigh mountains;
what the world gives back—
pebbles smoothed by tide,
a pinecone's dry geometry.

Sometimes it feels like wind chasing the small dust
in the hollow of a hill, or a dropped bucket
that spills. To catch and lose through touch—a hand
remembers what it was shaped to hold.

Only surface: the curve of a shell's lip,
a rust-flaked nail that once bound
two boards. Clenched then turned,
the palm expects.

Not empty—
open.
A bowl on a shelf;
a hand, waiting to be filled.

On the Downs

Walking the fields around the house,
like a water diviner
drawing futures in the air
with a willow switch.

I hear birds and squirrels.
On the chalk hills,
the trees grow in clumps
so they look like a single tree,

splitting into parts as I get closer.
The folded fungus
on the mossy branches is like
foamy waves breaking in the bay.

A round cob-stone has the same shape
as a tree stump, or even the copse
silhouetted on the horizon. As I lift it,
wood lice amble away reluctantly,
like soldiers off to war.

After a Storm, Fishermen Go Back to Sea

The wharf is still soaked grey
from the high waves.
Jetties stretch out
like the tines of a fork
pricking at the harbor waters.

The group splits
and makes ready,
telling old jokes
as they bale water from
below deck and tie back
lines loosened
by the storm.

Water churns,
and the scuppers spit.
There is a music in the lines,
hooks clattering
and ringing in the wind—
the slap of the waves.

The boats race
as they head out,
casting their eyes
to the horizon in hope
of a big haul.

Out with Her Husband at Dusk

There is a haze on the mild evening.
The grasses of the scarp slope slant
with the wind and there is thistle-down
in the air. The east slope is stained
fox-red as the low sun hits the gorse,

the shriveled stalks of bracken shine.
A skylark sings late in the season
and a heron barks. She jumps
across the stream, toes pointed, and
pirouettes as she lands. Her jacket

blows loose, three buttons come undone
on her blouse. Thoughts travel
like in a boat drifting away
from its moorings. She sees repeated,
one image frozen like a faded photograph—

a girl on a beach watching a sand tower
dissolve in the rising tide. She moves from
the centre of herself. As night comes the
moon lights the clouds, glowing ivory
in the dark sky. In the breeze the high grass

of the meadow shines like it was beaded
with dew. Their faces, whitened by the
moon, look like spirits. She walks
as far as the boundary gate. From there he
can follow the coast road down to the town.

Part 7:
Love That Passes By

Change of Season

Darkness has closed in
on the fields. The horizon shrinks.
From the outside, the farm glows
like embers in a fireplace.
I think of the moments we shared
in the blue of summer, how the winter is coming:
the warmth of the fire, the cold slap
of the waves when the rain comes.
The long night moves over.
The sounds are small. I follow the fence
up to the top ridge, across the meadow
through the torn wheat.
On the crest, there is a dog-fox
licking at the grass. It looks up
but does not scare. The cold air
touches gently.
Beneath the wavering edge of the horizon,
the outlines of the sheep in the far field.
Colours deepen in the bat-squeak
and moth-touch of the night.
As I look back, the stars are fastened
above the pale glow of the sea,
rounding the night beyond the boundary fences
and the dark trees.
I know he will not come back.

On the Beach

There are birds feeding out by the water's edge.
The sand dries white as my feet press. The hipped
and ruffled beach glows in the sun. All of what

I see is painted from the same closed
palette—beautiful as gods.
I watch a line of plovers on the warm beach,

pecking for food where the small waves
break. The birds are in a row, standing squat
as nuns on the way to prayer. The small

adjustments of their thin feet are charming
to me. They scuttle for sandflies that come
up roused by the cold and the sting of the foam;

or for little shrimps, pale as glass, pushed up by
the waves. Their short bills hover just above
the sand, where the sea meets the land, where things

press. Scared up as I pass, the birds rise—
suddenly beautiful as they take to the wing,
then settle again on the blue fringe of the shore.

The Season Changes

Walking away from the dark house,
along the hedges and close fields,
I come face to face with a fox. It stops—
pale red—as sunlight strikes across
the shoulders of the sycamores.
Looking at me, it moves along the stones
of an old boundary wall, patterned
white and orange with lichen.

There are flies around a cow pat,
the smell of leaves, and the sharp iodine
of salt spray carried up on the breeze,
from the sea.

A spring emerges from the foot of the scarp,
making a shallow pond of clear water
caught with weed. I follow the path
around it, under the cool shadow
of hedgerow trees.

A crow sits on the blond end
of a sawn stump. Winter touches gently.
The bees and wasps are mostly gone.
The air is crisp.

No longer warm on my face,
the sun is still bright.
I will not stiffen to the cold
or cling like the last leaf on the maple.

Who Has No Land Has No Sea

*Mare's tails and mackerel scales make
lofty ships carry low sails*
—Old Weather Proverb

That is how it is:
she sees only storms.
Getting the feed ready
for the ewes in the high
meadow, she thinks how
it was before he left.
A robin is standing on the
woodpile, looking for bugs in
the ragged tunnels of cut wood.
She hangs the laundry to dry—
the pegs stand up like birds.
The henhouse is broken,
its shingle roof bows and
the eaves are rotted. A shirt
flaps next to her knickers.
The sea calls her.

*

She swims out. Her body twists
as the sun catches the turn of her
muscles, the arc of her reach.
She leans into the water, diving
deep into a wave. Her lungs stretch.
Each stroke takes her further out.
She arches and turns, her belly
flat above the water for a moment.

The shore is a thin strip
of white. This is as far as she has
ever been. She has got here
quickly, as if she had wings
in the water. The sea feels pillowed,
like a bed. She does not hear
the beat of her heart. Water is
breath around her as she dives,
pushing handfuls away.
The sea is brown with silt. Deeper,
it clears. Forests of kelp, thick
as oil-cloth, brush against
her legs. The light is too thin for shadows.
She circles the seabed uncertain
how to touch, what to look for
in the gloom.

*

She lies on the beach, eating
blackberries from the thin brambles
in the slack. They have got sweeter
since last week, warmed by the sun.
Mare's tails are up in the sky and
wind is up, blowing the sand over
the dunes in thin ribbons. The tide draws
a silver line as her footprints vanish.

Late Spring. New Town

I walk down the coast road like a drum roll, over the litterings of sticks and bits of wood. The storm has brought down mud from the fields that stains the tarmac yellow. There are thin clouds. Everything is clear in the filtered light. The grass clicks as it springs back.

The limestone cottage is weathered to grey-green. I think about all the lives that it has seen. In the shadows, under edges—time hangs and rolls and floats. How the furniture of a life captures memories left in small dust. And none of us can say what stays and what we leave behind?

I walk to the port. There is a square and a church. On the harbor the boats are moored, the fenders knock together in the swell. Fishermen mend their nets, and some sleep on them in the low sun. There is a cafe, and in the warm evening all life is here spilling out into the streets. Girls walk arm in arm, and the boys try to look tough and pretend not to notice them. The old men smoke, and drink brandy out of sherry glasses.

The shadows are long on the sand as I walk along the beach. The day is still warm. I have been swimming and the salt pricks on my arms and belly as the seawater dries. I pick up a striped conch shell that has washed up on the beach. I hold it to my ear to hear the echoes of the sea.

Sputter

waking early
in my small white house
to listen for the quiet train
that I won't catch
this time
  or ever

the whistle
takes me out
on its metal way
and fades
  then stops

something like every break
that was ever in a song
or how dreams get carried off
  by the waking day

a candle flame
that rises up
  before it dies

one tooth
one syllable
my words
spinning away
  like leaves on the breeze

A Young Mother Tells a Story to Her Daughter Who Cannot Sleep for the Sound of the Waves on the Beach

The king of the sky looked down on the oceans and saw how the realm of the sea was flourishing and happy. He grew jealous to see the great whale breaking through the luminescence, and all the teeming life deep beneath the surface. Even at the bottom of the deepest ocean trench he saw the bug-eyed flashing fish with their fabulous luminous lures.

In anger, he sent down storms and raging seas that lasted a year. He had the gulls whisper and gossip that all the havoc and madness was because the queen of the sea had lost her love for her realm, and had grown careless and vain.

So, the queen of the sea was abandoned by all the creatures who lived under the water and she bore herself away with all the grace and fortitude she could muster, for she had a forgiving and adventurous spirit.

She went out of the sea and took off her robes of silver, and threw away her golden weapons. Like an actor when the play is finished, she left quickly and walked out of her part. She dressed herself in simple clothes and the noble lustre left her eyes.

On a shingle beach beaten by waves she slept with only sharp rocks as a pillow. The moon floated on the current and the tide carried the stars.

In this new realm she became a wanderer. She searched for a new life, treading a dusty pattern on the road's grey face and leaving footprints over the yellow arm of a long beach.

She found a new sea on the land. She did not mourn for all that she had lost. She listened well to the people she met.

They took her in and loved her.

With what pleasure and delight did she see flower petals whirl away in the wind like snow, and the hanging raindrops on the colored leaves of the maple. She looked to gather all the good of the Earth like a farmer at harvest time.

Then, one morning, like a bird she was gone away. Always holding the land in her heart, she returned to the water and vowed to win back the love of all the things that were in the sea, and to be a queen again. And the sea shone gold with her light.

About the Author

Kris Spencer is a teacher and writer based in London. His previous two collections, *Life Drawing* (2022) and *Contact Sheets* (2024), are published by Kelsay Books. His debut novel, *Every Storm is a Message,* is due for publication in 2025 by Holand Press.

www.ingramcontent.com/pod-product-compliance
Lightning Source LLC
Chambersburg PA
CBHW030051170426
43197CB00010B/1478